# REBUILDING YOUR LIFE

## —————AFTER A—————

## DIVORCE/BREAKUP

### THE DIVORCE LAWYER'S PERSPECTIVE

Shamika T. Askew, Esq.

# TABLE OF CONTENTS

I would like to dedicate this book to my parents —
John Henry Coon, Jr. and Vanessa Denise Askew. You both did your best to raise me to become the woman I am today. For that, I am eternally grateful to call you Daddyooooo and Mommy! Thank you for your love and continuous support. Love you forever and always!

Your baby girl,

*Mika*

# AUTHOR'S NOTE

To my audience: I am proud of you! You have purchased this book because you are facing or have recently faced a divorce or breakup. You are looking for answers on how to get through your situation and make it to the other side —joy, happiness, fulfillment, etc. Kudos to you for investing in yourself. I pray and hope that you find this book relatable and inspiring.

My biggest challenge in writing this book was making sure that I could write it in a way that would impact at least one man's or woman's life. I had so much anxiety and fear about whether anyone would relate to it. It took years to sit down and put my thoughts to paper. The impostor syndrome was out of this world as I wrote the manuscript, but I pushed past my fears as a new author. I hope that you find this book helpful. After reading it, I would appreciate your honest feedback.

While writing this book, I felt the need to ask you if you know Christ. If your answer is no, I would like you to consider accepting Christ as your Lord and Savior. It's very simple—just confess with your mouth that you believe in the Lord Jesus and believe in your heart that God raised Jesus from the dead, and you will be saved. This is according to Romans 10:9 (English Standard Version). There is no pressure to accept Christ. My life has been completely transformed because of Him, and I would be remiss if I didn't share the good news with you. I never want to leave people out of the loop from receiving "Good News."

I developed my personal relationship with God during my separation and divorce. Looking back, I can honestly say I didn't have an intimate relationship with God before that time. I was just a devout churchgoer.

In the midst of my separation and divorce, I asked God to send someone to help me on this journey because it was a lot to bear. I promised God that I would fast for three days until He sent someone to speak with me. God answered my prayers, and my life has not been the same.

Lastly, I'm confident that God told me to write this book because men and women need to hear from me about rebuilding their lives after a divorce or breakup. Some of you feel stuck and don't know how to escape the rut, but your life will never be the same from this day forward! How can I say that? Because I have the power to speak *LIFE* into *DEAD* situations. I want to speak *LIFE* into men and women who believe that their situations are *DEAD AFTER A DIVORCE OR BREAKUP.* And guess what? You have that same ability too! Your divorce/breakup will *NOT KILL YOU! YOU WILL BOUNCE BACK* from this storm/situation. I promise you! Believe that you will make it through and trust the process!

# I. WHY DID I WRITE THIS BOOK

## Why Did I Write This Book, and Who Is This Book For?

The short answer is that I am tired of seeing broken families. For some of us, the chaos, the confusion, the drama, the toxicity, and the dysfunction are all we know. We have literally become addicted to these types of environments. A family that is loving, caring, peaceful, respectful, happy, healed, healthy, and whole is hard to imagine when you've grown up in a dysfunctional environment.

I wrote this book because I am passionate about empowering both men and women to find solace during and after their divorce. I desire to see men and women thrive after experiencing a divorce/breakup and rebuild their lives. But, this book is not only for people experiencing a divorce or those who have divorced; it is also for individuals who were never married but went through a breakup after having children. If any of these situations sound like yours, then this book is for YOU!

## This Book Is Not Written in a Linear Manner. Whatever Chapter Speaks to You on a Particular Day, Start There! This is Not a Test!

If you are experiencing a separation, divorce, or have recently divorced, I am sure that your thoughts are constantly racing, and it's hard for you to focus.

I outlined this book in a fashion that allows you to read the chapter that speaks to you on a particular day. There may be some days when you need to read the same chapter twice. Allow yourself to process the information, process how you feel, and be reminded that you are not alone. Many of us share your experience, so there is no need to feel ashamed or like damaged goods. After completing this book, you will feel healed, happy, empowered, more inspired, and whole!

## My Personal Journey and Self-Discovery

I was born and partly raised in Detroit, Michigan. My parents were not married. In fact, many children in my neighborhood came from single-parent households. My parents had a very unhealthy relationship. To be honest, as a kid, I never understood how they had me because they didn't seem to like one another.

Although we didn't live together, my dad would visit me often. During most, if not all, of those visits, my parents would argue. One time, when I was roughly seven years old, I recall being really sick. I was literally vomiting with my head hovering over the toilet. Both of my parents were in the restroom with me; they were positioned on both sides of me—my dad to my left and my mom to my right.

I don't remember what started it, but they just started arguing right in front of me. I remember yelling at both of them and saying, "Really, I don't feel good!"

Unfortunately, in my home, this was my norm as a child. This type of unhealthy dialogue and relationship was the beginning of my exposure to confusion, toxicity, and—as a child—what I thought was LOVE.

As I journeyed through life, I found myself in these same environments. My puppy love relationship mirrored that of my parents'—very dysfunctional and unhealthy. It entailed a lot of arguing and sometimes even physical altercations. My first marriage also directly reflected what I was accustomed to as a child. As much as my former partner and I desired to have a healthy and whole marriage, we could not figure it out. As a result, the marriage dissolved, which left me with additional trauma to unpack and learn to heal from.

In 2019, at the age of thirty-four years young, I found myself, a divorce lawyer, in divorce court litigating my own divorce. I represented myself from start to finish. I can't say that I was completely shocked that my marriage was ending. The marriage was rocky from the very beginning, and as young adults, at ages twenty-one and twenty-three, we had no clue what we signed up for when we decided to marry.

## Desire to See Healthy, Healed, and Whole Families

While in law school, I recall having a keen desire to practice family law. I sat front row in every family law class, ready to take copious notes. My purpose in practicing family law was to save all of the children who had experienced pain and trauma from their childhood — similar to me.

If I could simply speak some sense into these parents as a family lawyer, I thought, then maybe more children would not have to suffer at the hands of their parents like I did. Boy, was I overly optimistic! I didn't realize how many other households operated similarly to the dysfunctional home I grew up in. Although I signed up to divorce people, I had a secret desire to practice family law to help create healthy, healed, and whole families. I can't tell you how many times I encouraged my clients to figure it out and seek counseling to save their marriage.

This book was birthed out of my desperation to see a change in the world. I'm a firm believer in being the change that I desire to see. I hope that I can impact many lives and help create a better place for us all—one household at a time.

# AFFIRMATION

I will have a healthy, healed, and whole family.

My previous relationships are my past, and I will not be bound by them.

From this day forward, my life will never be the same.

I will be more stable in my thoughts.

I will be clearer in my vision.

I will live and not die.

I will become stronger each day.

I will become the best version of myself, and so will my child(ren).

Not only will I survive this divorce or breakup, but I will thrive.

# II. WHO ARE YOU?

## Who Are You?

Some of us get into relationships and completely lose our identities. Others may identify who they are based on their titles or positions. And still, some of us never knew who we were prior to entering into a relationship.

Whatever category you find yourself in, the most important thing is discovering YOU after your divorce or breakup! So, who are you? As you begin to process the answer to this question, I want you to refrain from identifying yourself based on someone else's image or perception of you. Rather, I want you to focus on how you identify yourself.

Identity is commonly defined as "the set of qualities, beliefs, personality traits, appearance, and/or expressions that characterize a person or a group." I imagine that most of us began to develop our identity based on what we saw in our households as well as what our peers depicted. To be completely transparent, I took on the beliefs and qualities that were acceptable and pleasing to my parents and church members.

If you were dressed modestly, were studious, and well-behaved, you would be praised for being a great child. What child doesn't like being praised? Unfortunately, as I grew older, I attempted to portray this "perfect girl" image even more. By the time I reached my thirties, my life was starting to fall apart, and the perfect image that I was attempting to uphold began to crumble.

What happened to make my perfect life and image fade? First, it was going to jail for domestic violence. Second, my divorce came. I could no longer pretend to be the perfect girl. Most of my close friends and family had no clue that my marriage was rocky. At that time, I couldn't fathom sharing how imperfect I was and how I didn't have it all together. Why? Because at that stage of my life, I was everyone's go-to person.

After the jail incident and the divorce, life forced me to do some deep soul-searching. I had to look in the mirror and really ask myself, Who are you, Shamika? Who are you really? To be honest, I struggled with this question for a very long time. For most of my life, I was caught in an identity crisis, as I had to live up to the expectations of the church and my mother.

When I realized that it was OK to not be perfect or have everything figured out,

I was already thirty-plus years old and still searching for answers. At that phase of my life, I knew I was loving and caring, although I didn't always show it when upset. I loved to help people, even if it was to my detriment. I loved to have a good time, though I would feel guilty for not always being in work mode. I followed the rules despite seeing others succeed by bending or violating them. The point is that I have fought to figure out who I really was outside of my external influences.

One thing you may discover in life is that you have taken on beliefs or habits that were never truly yours, rather, they came from your former partner. I came to this conclusion while shopping at IKEA. During this time, I was in the separation phase of my life.

While I was walking around the store, I realized that I didn't enjoy shopping there at all. In fact, I hated that place. I realized that whenever my former spouse asked me to go to IKEA with him, I would always hesitate because it was my least favorite place to visit. I went because I wanted to enjoy his company. Looking back, it all makes sense now— IKEA was one of his preferred stores, not mine.

As you journey through your new life, you will begin to realize that you have taken on thoughts, beliefs, and insecurities that no longer suit you. I encourage you to find the real you; find the beliefs and thoughts that suit who you are now. It's OK to make changes to who you once were.

So, I need you to discover the new you. You are not the same man or woman you were when you got into that relationship. You have evolved. As you complete this book, I want you to take note of the old you versus the new you. Then, take some time to process the changes you've made for the better. There may be some things that still need improvement, and that's OK too. Just keep learning and growing.

As I approach my 40th birthday on December 7, 2024, I am more aware of who I am and what I desire out of life. I am an uplifter, motivator, encourager, supporter, loyal friend, worshiper, giver, snack eater, passionate lawyer, R&B lover, caring family member, traveler…the list goes on.

I had to discover this woman after many failed relationships, including my marriage. She was there the entire time, but my divorce led me to her. Most of us hate hardships, but it's the hardships that propel us into our greatness if we allow them to do so.

So, who are you?

## Your Job Doesn't Define You!

Your job is just a job. Once you leave that job, it will only be on your resume and nothing more. Our job titles do not define who we are; it's just a part of what we do. Some of us already know this, but then there are others who suffer from identity issues because their identity is their job title. We all have encountered this sort of person. To be frank, this was my problem when I was in my twenties.

I had severe image issues. I didn't have an identity outside of wanting the title of "lawyer." Luckily, by the time I became a lawyer, I really didn't care about the title anymore. The point is to find yourself outside of your work. When people ask you to tell them about yourself, don't lead with your job title or job description; tell them who you are outside of work.

## Your Role in a Household Doesn't Define You!

During my divorce process, I realized that I never knew who I was. I was twenty-three years old when I got married. Looking back, I had no business getting married because I was still learning about life, let alone marriage. I was not in the position to be a wife. I didn't understand the concept of a wife, nor did I have healthy examples of marriage growing up.

I got married because it seemed like the next societal step after graduating from college. At age twenty-three, I was definitely influenced by the so-called social norms. At that age, society says you should be done with college and preparing to marry and have children. I fell right into that rabbit hole.

These are some of the societal pressures that women often experience. Although I am not a man, I can imagine that men also feel the pressure to conform to social norms, as they are often looked at as primary providers in their relationships, even though they have so much more to offer. Women are not just homemakers, and men are not just financial providers. It's our job to show people who we are outside of these roles. If you are not appreciated for the intangibles that you have to offer someone, then perhaps you would be better suited elsewhere.

## How Do You Determine Your Worth?

In divorce cases with property, sometimes appraisers are hired to give a valuation of the marital property. They compare data against the subject property to determine its true cost. Have you ever realized that we sometimes operate under this same methodology? For example, if a man has an affair and his woman finds out, the woman usually finds herself comparing her looks, educational level, possessions, etc., to the other woman.

She literally begins to measure her worth against the other woman. It is so disheartening that we have come to this point as a people. I don't believe that our worth was ever intended to be measured by these things.

As a child, I remember my dad would always tell me that the prettiest woman on earth could be the ugliest because of her nasty attitude. That always stayed with me. So, growing up, I did my best to have a fun and vibrant attitude because I didn't want to be considered ugly.

From my observation, most women appear to value themselves based on their appearance, their educational success, and their possessions. And with men, they seem to value themselves based on their income, their cars, and their sexual performance. Now, this list is obviously not exhaustive, but you get the picture. We were never created to value ourselves based on superficial systems.

People will remember us more for our acts of service rather than if we had the latest and greatest fashion items or vehicles. I hope that we begin to value ourselves based on more meaningful things, such as serving others in need, showing acts of kindness to all genders, races, and statuses, and impacting the community with good deeds.

# AFFIRMATION

I was chosen by the creator to put a mark on this earth.

There is no one on earth like me.

I am unique and special.

I am not defined by my household roles or job title(s).

I have self-worth.

I am valuable.

I am more than enough.

# III. LOVE

## Love

Everyone wants to be loved by someone. The problem is that I'm not sure if we really know how to love unconditionally. I can't tell you how many times I have heard clients and potential clients tell me they "fell out of love." I asked them, "How is that possible?" The general response is that their significant other doesn't make them happy anymore.

What is so interesting about this statement is that most people get married because their partner makes them happy. Ironically, they come and see me because their partner is making them unhappy. So, I wonder, should the feeling of happiness or unhappiness be grounds for marrying or divorcing? Personally, I don't think so, but thousands of people have divorced for this reason. The bigger goal is to figure out what love is to us.

## What Is It?

Personally, I can't put a concrete definition on love. I just know how it feels when I receive it. It makes me feel like I can be my genuine self, I feel accepted, I feel reassured, I feel heard, I feel wanted, etc. I can tell you that when I receive it, I desire it often because love is beautiful. I love, love, love to be loved, and I love to give love.

What is it to you? How does it make you feel? You need to be aware of it so you can begin to attract it.

## Let's Start Loving YOU First

If I had to guess, I would bet top dollar that you have not been loving you FIRST. You have poured into your partner, your job, your kids, your family, your friends, and then whatever is left, if anything, is what you give to yourself. Well, my friend, we are changing that today. We will learn to put ourselves first, and yes, I know some of you suffer from mommy/daddy guilt, but your children need to have a complete, healthy, and whole parent.

You are a much better parent when you are healthy. You are healthy when you are loved adequately and often. So, start by getting your planner out and marking self-care on the calendar. This is too important to miss.

## Let's Water You Because You Deserve It

I'm not sure where it came from, but I have struggled over the years with feeling like I don't deserve great things. I love to celebrate other people and even give my time and talents to the people I care about. The times when people have tried to give to me, I politely decline or even start questioning if I should accept their generosity. As I have traveled on my self-love journey, I have come to realize that it is because I am so used to giving so much of myself and not having many people give back to me. It feels foreign having people do for you when you are normally the one giving to others.

In 2023, I decided to start loving myself. And, I promised myself that I would not feel bad about it either. My motto for 2023 was "Loving on me, all 2023." The love that I so desperately wanted to give to my husband, my friends, and my family, I began giving to myself.

I made sure that my hair, nails, and toes were done. I began texting myself inspirational messages. I treated myself to nice meals and luxury items. Doing these things made me realize that I had never really loved on myself before. While it was a sad realization, I was eager and determined to correct my mistakes.

I'm sure this is the story for some of you. I challenge you to start loving on yourself. Think of yourself as a plant. A plant needs to be watered often and receive enough sunlight; otherwise, it will die. So, today, you will begin to water yourself by pouring into your own cup and you will get sunlight by doing the things that you love, ensuring your plant flourishes!

# AFFIRMATION

I am an intentional lover.
Love is all around me.
I love to love.
I love to be loved.
I am worthy of a healthy love.
I deserve to be loved.
I am the most important person in my life.
I matter to me.
I love myself.

# IV. YOU ARE NOT A FAILURE

If no one has told you, let me be the first to say that you are not a failure! As children, we grow up getting letter grades in school and quickly attach our worth to our grades. The truth of the matter is that these performance tests start from birth. Think about it: when you first learned to walk, crawl, ride a bike, etc., you had someone clapping and cheering you on. Then, you started school and began taking tests. If you did well on the test and received great grades, you felt amazing. The same is true—when you bombed your test, you felt horrible.

Society has taught us to attach our worth to almost everything. I'm here to tell you to STOP! I'm speaking to myself as well. I am not a failure because my marriage failed!

## The Marriage Failed

A failed marriage is a hard pill to swallow for anyone; trust me, I know from first-hand experience. Even as I type these words, I am reminded of the pain. You change your mindset that the marriage was not successful because two individuals could not learn how to effectively communicate and solve problems together. It feels less bad, at least that's what I've told myself and would like to believe. I do believe that there is some truth to this.

Most people only seek marriage counseling at the start of the marriage or when things go bad. In my eight years of practicing family law, I always ask people, "What have you done to save the marriage?" The response is usually that they went to counseling, but counseling didn't work.

I've never heard anyone tell me they invested in their marriage by taking classes and courses on communicating, budgeting, team building, etc. Think about it: some (not all) jobs that desire to see their employees succeed send their employees to obtain significant training. The purpose is to ensure that the employee has everything that is needed to be successful at the job.

I'm just wondering why we don't take that same approach to our marriages. The likelihood of your marriage being successful is far greater when there is an investment into making the marriage great. I'm a firm believer that what you put into anything determines what you get out of it.

Marriage takes work, and truthfully, most of us don't put everything into the marriage to make it successful. I know you believe that you did, but unless you can show me the certificates you obtained from communicating, resolving high-conflict matters, and team-building skills, I would confidently say you didn't give it 100%. Neither did I. I wanted to, but it takes two people to want the marriage to work. Perhaps that was your scenario as well.

You are not your marriage. The marriage failing was something that happened to you, but it certainly does not define you!

## Stop Carrying the Shame

If you grew up in church, as I did, then marriage is the second most important thing that a young adult could do after getting saved. From my experience, if you were not married by twenty-five, then something had to be wrong with you. That's the message I received growing up, whether that was the intent or not.

The church didn't want young people fornicating, so they told us that it was better to "marry than to burn." As a young adult, you don't want to "burn" for eternity for simply having a desire to have sex. So, what did some of my generation of church friends do? We got married.

Unfortunately, it was also the church that made me feel horrible for filing for divorce. The church took on the position that I should stay in an unhealthy and toxic relationship while knowing that my husband found "greener grass." I sought God for myself and truly believed that God released me from that marriage since my partner had no intent on returning home. Once I received God's approval, I didn't care what the church had to say. Admittedly, I walked around with a lot of shame for filing for divorce, but I knew that I had legal grounds, according to the Bible, to file for divorce, so I did.

Most people know that divorce rates are high, but for some strange reason, we still feel ashamed that our marriage didn't work, as if half the people on earth who ever married didn't also experience a divorce. Contrary to some people's beliefs, being a divorcée does not make us damaged goods. There is absolutely nothing to be ashamed about. If you know that you did the best you could and it simply did not work, then have peace and release yourself from the guilt and shame of other people's opinions about YOUR LIFE!

# AFFIRMATION

I am not a failure.
I am not damaged goods because of my failed relationships.
I am worthy of relationships with substance.
I am not ashamed of my story.
My story will create generational wealth for my family and me.
Why not me?
I am not defeated.
I WIN!

# V. FORGIVENESS

## Forgive Yourself

Have you forgiven yourself yet? If not, now is the perfect opportunity to tell yourself that you are sorry for hurting YOU! You probably forgave everyone else except the most important person—YOU! It's time that you learn to forgive yourself for every past mistake.

No one has a manual on how to do life. There is a lot of trial and error that comes with living. The fact that you made it this far is a testament in itself. Today, you will move forward with a clean slate, knowing that you are allowed to make mistakes, but you will learn from them.

One of my favorite sayings is, "When you know better, you do better." A lot of us didn't know any better when we entered into our marriages or long-term relationships. Now that we are separated or divorced, we have so much relationship experience under our belts that we will do better the next time. I like to call my first marriage "my practice marriage." They say practice makes perfect!

## Forgive Your Partner

One of my life coaching assignments during my separation and divorce was to write several letters. One of the letters had to be written to my former spouse. In the letter, I explained to him that I wasn't upset about him abandoning me, leaving me with our household bills, and lying about praying for our marriage during the separation when, in fact, he wasn't praying for our marriage; he was living his best life.

I explained to him how hurt I was that someone whom I had been married to for over ten years could treat me this way. I explained to him that I completely lost trust in a lot of people after he showed me the ill side of what a life partner could do. I told him that he didn't have to go searching for greatness outside of our marriage because greatness was always within him. I forgave him for what he did to me, and most importantly, I apologized for the hurt and pain I caused him.

I re-read the letter again before writing this chapter. The letter was written on September 7, 2019, and emailed to him on September 11, 2019. The best part about the letter was when I wrote this: "I can honestly say that now, I am so happy that you left me because without you leaving, I would not have discovered my worth, my confidence, my ability to get wealth, and most importantly. . . God." Five years ago, I had no idea how powerful this statement would be. I knew that I would be fine, but picking up the pieces of your broken heart and moving forward can be challenging. Now that I'm on the other side, I am so grateful for the journey.

## It's OK to Grieve

When people say that divorce feels like death. . . they are not lying. For the first several months of my separation, I promise it felt like I was going through a drug detox. I have never been on drugs in my life, but you cannot convince me that I wasn't experiencing a detox from the toxic marriage.

Even as bad as it was, it was my life for over ten years. I needed my "fix." It felt like someone was ripping my heart out of my chest. There were days that I could not breathe, and it felt like I was suffocating. The hardest part of the first few months was not communicating with my ex because he blocked me from being able to call or text. I was only able to communicate via email.

The grieving process was insane because the control freak (me) was not able to be in control. He had all control at this point. He controlled when we spoke and when we didn't. He left on February 2, 2019, and by September 2019, when I wrote the letter to him, I had done all of my grieving. I realized that the marriage was over and that my life would actually be much better without being married to him.

Your grieving process is your journey. Don't compare your healing process by how long it took others to move on. Everyone grieves and heals at their own pace. Some people move on without dealing with their pain—there is no set time limit. And for goodness' sake, do not look to your former partner as a guide on how quickly she/he has moved on.

From my personal observation, men seem to move on quicker than women. In some of my divorce cases, the ink hadn't dried on the paperwork before the male clients were already with a new girlfriend or fiancée. There is absolutely no judgment. You should solely focus on your grieving process. When you feel the time is right to move forward, then you will.

## Grace

When I think of grace, I think of unlimited forgiveness. It doesn't matter what I've done wrong; I am forgiven for mistake after mistake. In this phase of your life, it's so important to operate in grace. My focus is for you to give yourself as much grace as possible. Sometimes, it feels like the world is against you, but if there is one person who needs to have your back after God, it should be you. Nobody will have your best interest like you. You may stumble on this journey of rebuilding your life, but keep getting back up, no matter how many times you think you have failed.

# AFFIRMATION
## Look in the mirror

I forgive you, (insert your name).
You are appreciated.
I am sorry for not making you feel important.
You matter most to me.
I will be more kind to you.
I will give you the grace that I give to others.
I forgive my former partner (insert his/her/their name).
I release any anger, hurt, and resentment towards him/her/them.

# VI. POWER

## Have You Recognized the Power Within You?

I firmly believe that most of us fail to recognize the power that lies within us. I can confidently say that if we truly recognized this power, it would be impossible for others to easily control or manipulate us. Please understand that while you may not recognize the power within yourself, your perpetrators do. You are capable of fulfilling anything that you put your mind to. There is nothing that you can't accomplish! Once you start to recognize your power and begin to walk in it, you will be UNSTOPPABLE!

## Power Trip

As a divorce lawyer, I see the games that are played over and over again. One party, if not both, is in a power struggle. Both want to gain power over the other. This was likely the case during the marriage and/or relationship and is usually the case during the divorce/legal proceeding and after the initial legal proceedings (such as modification proceedings where you want to adjust the parenting plan or child support).

It's almost as if one party or both parties want to treat the other like a puppet. Once the party falls into the trap, the game continues to be played. Some fall for the trap over and over again. For context, this could look like one party constantly blowing up your phone or emails. The party doing all of the calling and/or texting is solely trying to gain control over the situation in an attempt to force the other to respond to their demands expeditiously. The other party (the one receiving all of the calls or text messages), if they don't know the game that is being played, will get flustered and shut down.

The goal of the game is to WEAR YOU OUT until you give in to their demands. Recognize the game and stop responding how you normally respond. I know this happens often because this behavior continues once the court case begins. If the party doing all the calling or texting does not have a lawyer, then I can easily speak directly to these individuals. Normally, they treat me the same way. I have learned to only respond to what is necessary. Their game is to see me get flustered and engage with their nonsense.

When you don't engage how they want you to act, then they can't control the scenario. I would recommend that you only respond to questions that require a response. This could be questions concerning the child/children's safety, schooling, or well-being.

## Take Your Power Back

Stop giving up your power! You have allowed your former partner or soon-to-be former partner to control your moods for far too long. No one should be able to dictate your mood. You have complete control over your thoughts and your emotions, so stop giving someone else the power to control you.

Control your actions—don't be used as a puppet or allow yourself to be tossed to and fro. You are not a puppet. You are better than that. You are an amazing human being with lots to offer the world, so please start acting like it! Dig deep within to find your strength and ignore the tactics being used by your former partner or soon-to-be former partner.

## Show Up, Even When You Don't Feel Like It

When I was growing up, I developed a habit of frequently dressing up and looking nice. It didn't matter where I was going; I wanted to make an impression. I did this even if I was having a bad day. In fact, I tried to look extra pretty on those bad days because I needed to feel good internally.

As I continued to mature, I discovered that this is a great trait to have. Forcing yourself to get dressed and show up even when you don't feel like it will cause you to start feeling good because you look good. No one can debunk the fact that when you look good on the outside, you start to feel good on the inside.

Some of you have been in bed and struggled just to wash your face and brush your teeth. Depression has set in and has taken control of your day-to-day activities. Well, that will end TODAY! You will no longer be in this rut, and you will start to take complete control of your day.

I need you to get out of bed, get dressed, get your haircut, or get your hair done, then go somewhere. . . anywhere, even if it's to the grocery store. You need to be SEEN. While you are out, I bet you will get a ton of compliments on your appearance, which will make you feel extra special. There's something about being complimented—it triggers something in everyone.

## Obsession – Just STOP

When I work on family law cases—whether it is a divorce or a custody case, there is a part of the process called discovery. Essentially, it's when lawyers exchange documents to determine if they have a good case based on the evidence presented by both sides. In family law, we are fighting over children and money. However, when it comes to the money, usually, some parties become detectives and go into overdrive in analyzing their partner's bank transactions. They become obsessed with all of the information that they receive, and it leads them into a rabbit hole. One piece of information leads them to another source, and then some even start to hack into their partners' email accounts to find more information.

My advice to individuals who have not gone through the entire divorce or custody process is to prevent yourself from being this person. If you suspect that your partner is cheating, then your intuition is probably right, no matter how many times your partner has denied it. If you start to analyze every bank transaction, you will drive yourself crazy.

## Letting Go of CONTROL – It's More Freeing Than You Think!

I remember, during my divorce process, I had a conversation with my life coach. I told him that it was challenging to give up control. It was to the point that I hated surprises because I wasn't in control of the details. I wanted to know everything. I would plan everything on my calendar because I could not live a life of spontaneity. Then, one day, I started being spontaneous, and it was life-changing. I felt more free giving up control rather than being in control. Now, this does not mean that you still don't plan for things, but for overthinkers like me, taking a step back and allowing things to happen organically can be beautiful.

I see this the most when clients need to know every single detail and the exact outcome of their case. Some clients, who are obsessed with being in control, may insist that I give them precise instructions for their situation, believing that if I make the decision for them, the outcome will be more favorable. I rarely tell clients what decisions to make. Most of the time, I give my clients options and allow them to decide what they believe is best. Now, of course, I can give them some guidance on what I have seen judges do in the past, but I emphasize to them that the judge has a broad discretion to make rulings, so their outcome could be different.

Not knowing the outcome of your divorce or custody case can be extremely scary. The best way to deal with this is to consider your best and worst days in court. If you can survive your worst day in court, then you are not in bad shape. If you can't survive your worst day in court, then settling your case is likely your best option.

For people like me, who struggle to let go, I want you to give this a try. Do your best to not control every single detail of your life. Leave a little room for things to come up. You will be surprised at how much we can actually miss out on—because we are too busy being laser-focused on the intricate details. It's OK not to know what will happen next. You will eventually find the beauty in the element of surprise. So, learn to let go and go with the flow!

# AFFIRMATION

I recognize the power within me.
I am a force to be reckoned with.
I am unstoppable.
I am fearless.
I let go of the need to be in control of everything.
I will recognize my opponent's strategies and tricks
and will not play their games.
I have the strength and power to make it through this challenge.

# VII. ACCOUNTABILITY

**Accountability** — owning up to your actions. Most people do not like being accountable. It's like pulling out a tooth to get most people to admit that they were wrong. Oh, and don't you dare ask for an apology for their actions that caused you harm; you would definitely be doing the most damage from their viewpoint. Why? Because they don't see that they've done anything wrong.

If you are waiting for your former partner or soon-to-be former partner to take accountability for their actions that led to the divorce or breakup, then you might be wasting your time. I don't want to focus on them, though. I'd much rather focus on you. It's time for you and I to look in the mirror and accept our part in the failure of our marriage/relationship.

## What Role Did You Play in Your Failed Marriage?

This is a crucial task for you to complete. Your former partner, or soon-to-be ex-partner, was not entirely responsible for the failure of the marriage or relationship. Most of you, not all, have experienced failed relationships before. With that being said, you have been the common denominator in all of your failed relationships. It's important for you to figure out what you could have done better in these relationships because our goal is to have healthy and whole relationships. However, this cannot be accomplished if you have the mindset that you are perfect and everyone else is to blame.

As hard as it was to accept, I had to come to the realization that I was the common denominator in all of my failed relationships. My biggest problem was my mouth—I would speak blessings, but I would also speak harsh words. Growing up, there was this rhyme that we used to sing as children – "sticks and stones may break my bones, but words will never hurt me." I do not know who authored this rhyme, but it's not the truth. Words hurt. Words cut deep.

At a young age, I became a master at using my words for good and bad. Unfortunately, I killed (figuratively, not literally) many people with my words. I could make the excuse that it was how I was raised and blah, blah, blah, but that wouldn't be acceptable. I had to dig deep to figure out why I wanted to hurt people with words. Once I realized that it's wrong to hurt others with words simply because I was in pain, I stopped doing so.

Bear in mind that a lot of our bad habits will not be resolved overnight. It will take time and regular interactions with people to truly test your patience and determine if you've grown. I knew that I was growing when I no longer desired to see people suffering because of my harsh words. It was toxic and very dark, to say the least.

Now, my desire is to express how people have hurt me or disappointed me, and if they don't listen and make a change for the better, then I just simply remove these people from my life. It's really that simple—there's no need to cut deep. They will feel the difference when my presence is no longer around. That's the space that I need you to be in. Not everyone has a good spirit and energy, and quite frankly, not everyone deserves to be in your presence. Be a better version of yourself and become selective of those who should be in your circle.

# AFFIRMATION

I accept full responsibility for the mistakes made in my failed relationships.
I will not make the same mistakes twice.
I acknowledge that I have hurt others and caused them pain.
I will seek healthy outlets to deal with my pain and anger.
I am a better person now than ever before.

# VIII. SHATTERED DREAMS

## Shattered Dreams

What does this even mean? Personally, it means that the dream of having a family was destroyed the day I divorced… at least, that's what I thought. When I was in my early twenties, I wanted to create the life that I didn't have growing up. I thought that if I were to get married and have children, my childhood trauma would disappear because I could just start fresh with my own little family. So, I got married and pregnant.

Deep down, I knew my marriage wouldn't succeed. But , I wanted to give it everything I had–to live the life I never knew. Although I would always verbally communicate with family and friends that I had a desire to be a successful lawyer and single mother, I always wanted a healthy and whole family. It was just difficult to verbalize this aspiration or even imagine having a healthy and whole family because I had never witnessed it. Having a healthy and whole family just never seemed to be within reach.

## You Didn't Have the Family You Desired

I didn't have the family that I desired with my first husband. When I got married at twenty-three, I didn't know what to expect as a wife since this was my first marriage. Growing up, I didn't see many examples of a healthy and loving marriage. Most of the marriages I saw were unhealthy or toxic. Even the healthy marriages that I witnessed underwent lots of abuse and suffering before the happy ending occurred. In addition, I didn't have much dating experience prior to getting married. The only dating experience I had was one other relationship, which was also toxic and unhealthy.

Throughout the years of my marriage, I remember crying and being frustrated on a weekly basis. This is no exaggeration. The marriage seemed to be doomed from the very beginning, but I'm not a quitter. I kept believing that things would change for the better. I recall having numerous conversations with close family members and friends about how my marriage was not "normal." I recall one friend asking me if anyone's relationship was normal. I responded in the affirmative. Although I didn't know exactly what a normal marriage looked like, I knew that mine wasn't one of them.

As I write this book in 2024, I am forever grateful that I didn't have the family that I desired with my first husband. Why? Because I would have repeated the same unhealthy and toxic cycle from my childhood. In February 2019, when my separation began, I thought that my life was over, and I didn't know what my future would look like. It's hard being optimistic when you are in the midst of your separation or divorce/breakup. Looking back, I can tell you that my life is just getting started!

## You Are Not Less Than (woman not bearing a child)

One of the most devastating moments during my divorce process was realizing that I never had my child. In 2014, I got pregnant. I had dreamed of becoming a mother since I was nineteen, so you can imagine how excited I was. As soon as I took the pregnancy test and received confirmation from the doctor, I began the planning process of being a mother. I also began to fantasize about what our family gatherings and trips would look like.

I'll never forget that day, it was April 2, 2014. I had a doctor's appointment scheduled. I was looking forward to this visit because we were supposed to hear the baby's heartbeat. I eagerly waited for the doctor to come into the room to begin the procedure. As we waited for the doctor, my former partner and I chatted about boy names and had already begun purchasing boy clothes, even though we didn't know the sex of the baby yet.

The doctor walked in, we smiled and greeted one another. Once the doctor turned on the ultrasound and began searching for the baby, it seemed like an eternity for the doctor to tell us about the baby and to hear the heartbeat. Then, the doctor said, "Unfortunately, I can't see the baby." It felt like the entire world stopped at that moment. I really didn't understand what that meant. A miscarriage was never in my thought process.

After asking the doctor what was happening, he explained to us that we were having a miscarriage. He then told me that I could allow the process to pass naturally at home. So, I got up, and we headed home. Once we arrived home, the cramps and bleeding began. I stayed in the bathroom and cried all night. All I could say was, "God, why?" Eventually, my grieving process got better, but I still get emotional about it. Even as I type these words, tears are flowing from my face, and it's been over ten years since the miscarriage.

## Create New Traditions

After a divorce/breakup, especially if children are involved, it can be difficult to plan for the future. As a divorce lawyer, I am often tasked with helping my clients create a parenting plan. This task is usually difficult for clients because it forces them to look past their present situation and focus on the future.

Most clients get stuck on how things have been or how things are going in the present. One of the things that I always do is speak into their lives and remind them that one day, they will remarry and will have new family traditions. This often comes up when we are discussing the school breaks for the children. I usually find that some clients want to split Thanksgiving Day or the Thanksgiving break along with Christmas break. I ask them, if you split Thanksgiving Day or Thanksgiving break or Christmas Day, then how are you going to travel with your new partner and children?

There is usually complete silence after asking this question. The clients who go along with me and find a little hope usually agree and don't split the break because they realize that it would be very difficult traveling if they have to return home to exchange the children with the other parent. The clients who like to have control over the other partner/parent (not always, just from my experience) tend to want to split Thanksgiving Day and Christmas Day because it ensures that the soon-to-be former partner cannot travel with the children.

If you are like me and didn't have children during the marriage, the divorce process is not as complex, but still very devastating. The second challenging post-divorce experience for me was traveling alone. My former partner and I grew up in Michigan, so we would travel from Florida to Michigan for the holidays.

After the divorce, I had to travel alone. I never thought that this would be an issue, but when you see husbands and wives with their families traveling during the holidays, it can be really sad. It was like that for me for the first year or so. After my divorce, I learned to create new traditions, which included traveling to new places, getting a pet to keep me company, and learning to do absolutely nothing.

## Your Divorce Was a Setup for Something GREATER

At this very moment, you probably can't see how great your life is going to be post-divorce/breakup, but let me tell you that your story gets BETTER! How do I know? Because a great person can't stay down in the dumps for too long. What I love most about us men and women is that hardships and challenges make us so much stronger and powerful.

This challenge of facing a divorce/breakup is no different than any other challenge that you have ever faced in life. To date, there has not been one challenge that has taken you out, not a single one! For this very reason, I am confident that this divorce/breakup will not take you out, either!

In 2019, when I divorced, I never thought that someday, I would be inspiring men and women to thrive after a divorce/breakup. At that time, I was living in my one-bedroom apartment, crying and watching YouTube videos on how other women made it through their divorce. Their stories always gave me hope that I could also make it to the other side. Approximately two months after my divorce was finalized, I decided to publish my personal divorce vlogs on YouTube.

My first video was published on my birthday, December 7, 2019. I thought, what better way to celebrate me than to rebrand my entire law firm and let everyone know that I was officially divorced? I decided to publish my personal divorce vlogs on YouTube because I knew how impactful other women's stories were to my life.

I need you to recognize how important your story is as well. The world needs to hear from you! There is a lack of men sharing their divorce stories, and other men need to hear about your healing journey. Your divorce was a steppingstone for you to accomplish and fulfill more on this earth. There's more to you than the 9 am-5 pm job or even your business.

Some of you have books, plays, podcasts, movies, songs, etc. We need to hear it. The best time to start is NOW! This is a great way to escape from the pain that you might be experiencing with this divorce/breakup process or even post-divorce. Think about it: our favorite artists put out their best work when they were experiencing hell at home! You are no different than our favorite artist. Let's get it done! I believe in you and want to hear about your journey!

# AFFIRMATION

My initial dreams may have been shattered, but I am picking up the
pieces and creating a new picture.
I will create new family traditions with new characters in my story.
I will bear a child, and I am not less than a woman for not having a child… yet.
My time is coming.
This divorce or breakup was a setup for me to GO GET IT.
I am thankful for the failed relationship(s) because
I did not know that I needed me more.
I will have the family that I desire.

# IX. TAKE YOUR TIME

## Take Your Time

As a divorce lawyer, I can't tell you how many times people try to rush the divorce process. By the time most people call the law office to start their divorce, they are ready to be divorced immediately. I have to kindly remind them that this process takes time, and that there are several factors that play a part in the process.

Most people have never been through a court proceeding, so it's definitely understandable to have high expectations. Unfortunately, I have to be the bearer of bad news and give people more realistic expectations. It's hard to hear that if your case is contested (in the event that you and your soon-to-be former partner do not agree to every issue in a divorce and have to seek the judge's intervention), then your divorce case can take a year or longer. The same is true in custody battles after a breakup.

Honestly, I didn't understand people's rush to end the marriage until I experienced my own divorce. For some reason, in my mind, the quicker the judge signs off on the divorce paperwork, the sooner the pain and agony will go away. I just wanted to feel happy and at peace again. I really thought that my peace of mind was connected to that piece of paper—the divorce final judgment.

Let me remind you that you can have peace DURING the divorce process. You don't need to wait until the paper is signed and sealed to find your peace! The peace you have access to can only be found within yourself. There is not a single person on earth or any tangible item that can bring you peace. I would encourage you to stop looking to people and things to bring you happiness and peace. The more you look to external things to bring you fulfillment, the more disappointed you are going to be.

## Your Timeline is Not the Ultimate Timeline

As I mentioned previously, when most people call law offices, they are ready for the divorce and are eager to expedite it. If you are in the divorce process, I kindly ask you to throw away your timeline of when you expect the case to be over. I can assure you that your timeline is likely inaccurate.

If you have gone through a divorce recently, then I kindly ask you to throw away your timeline of when you expect to feel free and at peace again. Both journeys are going to take time. Not only is it going to take time, but it will require some patience on your part.

One thing I've learned is that we, as humans, don't like to wait. We lack patience. We want everything fast and to have it our way. Your timeline will likely not be the final outcome, so please learn to be OK with that. The quicker you can grasp this, the better for you.

I can admit that I do not have a lot of patience, either. Quite frankly, I hate waiting. I want what I want and when I want it. So, you are definitely not alone. I can tell you that my divorce process frustrated me to the core. I could not understand why God would have me wait for it to be over.

## This is Not a Sprint

Getting to the divorce line as fast as possible should not be your goal. You will not win a trophy for making it to the finish line first. In my humble opinion, the goal should be embracing your circumstances and learning to be the best version of yourself as one chapter ends and a new chapter begins. Your new journey of being single, happy, healthy, and whole is just that—a journey!

My divorce situation was very unique. I started my divorce process in March 2019 when I filed it in court. After it was filed, I had my former partner served at work…on purpose. Initially, I started the divorce process because I was looking to get a reaction out of my former partner. I wanted him to feel the rejection that I felt when he left the marital home and didn't return.
At that time, I wasn't really ready for a divorce.

In May 2019, we started completing some of the paperwork and even signed a fully executed marital settlement agreement. The last step was to set the matter for an uncontested final hearing. As I began looking for hearing dates to finalize the divorce, I felt this tug within. I sensed that something was telling me to slow down, but I didn't know if this was my own personal thoughts or if this was God speaking to me.

On June 3, 2019, I asked God to give me clear direction on whether I should be moving forward with the final hearing. My specific prayer to God was to give me a sign by sending a messenger to tell me specifically what to do. I told God I would fast for three days since the number three seemed significant based on stories that I had read in the Bible.

On June 8, 2019, God answered my prayer in five days. He sent an old high school friend who I had not spoken to in years. My high school friend indicated that God spoke to him about me and my situation. He told me things that only God could have shared with him. He told me that God wanted me to pause the divorce because there were some things He wanted to show me.

The call with my high school friend lasted about an hour and a half. During the call, I received the clarity that I needed. From that moment, I realized that God was real and that my life would never be the same after that call. Because I believed that God orchestrated this call, not only did I pause the divorce, but I dismissed it. There was nothing more important to me than to be obedient to God.

Reflecting back to 2019, I am so grateful for the journey. What appeared to be a delay in my divorce process was actually God's way of showing me that He had a different path for me. I didn't know what the outcome was going to be. There were times when I thought that reconciliation would occur. Whether we reconciled or not, I was going to live my life. Eventually, I found that I was the most satisfying factor in my life.

I believe that most of us want to divorce quickly because we believed we had wasted so much time on the wrong person. So, we have to play catch up with the time. I hope that as you continue to read this book and journey through life, you recognize that your time will be redeemed and that you are exactly where you need to be. Even with the divorce, your life is still on the right track with time.

# AFFIRMATION

I am exactly where I am supposed to be.
I am not behind, but right on time.
I will not get fixated on how long it takes for things to happen in my life.
Life is not a sprint.
I am running my own race and staying in my lane.

# X. DIVORCING WITH CHILDREN: HEALTHY CO-PARENTING

## Divorcing With Children: Healthy Co-Parenting

If you are anything like me, the term "healthy co-parenting" may at first seem impossible. However, I realized that just because I was a product of an unhealthy environment does not mean my future has to look like my past. I have the power to create a different life than what I have been accustomed to.

What does healthy co-parenting even mean? To me, it looks like the opposite of what I experienced as a child. It looks like a home with little to no arguing, no cursing, no fighting, etc. It looks like healthy dialogue and conversations where adults agree to disagree. It looks like a household where the parents love their children more than they hate each other.

A healthy co-parenting environment will have a tremendous impact on your new life and the child(ren). The happier, healthier, and whole you are, the better you will be at work, for your family, and, most importantly, for your children.

Please make it a goal to put every effort into being the best co-parent you can be to your children. As much as we like to shield our children from harm, the divorce or breakup will have an impact on them. It's our responsibility to do our best to aid them in their healing journey as you heal as well.

## Communication Between Parents

Depending on how badly the divorce or breakup ended will determine the form of communication used between the co-parents. At least, that has been my experience as an attorney. It appears that when parents have a healthier co-parenting relationship, they are willing to communicate directly on their cell phones—via calls and text. However, the unhealthier co-parenting relationships require a co-parenting app such as Talking Parents or Our Family Wizard.

Whatever communication method you decide to use, it is important to ensure you are communicating as effectively as possible and showing respect to the other co-parent. I can't tell you how many times I have to review messages for a hearing, and there is a lot of disrespect within the messages. Or, better yet, there is one parent telling the other parent what they should or should not be doing as if they were the child.

It doesn't matter where you are; your approach always matters. Most of us would never speak to our superiors how we speak to the mother or father of our child.

It's understandable that the dynamics of the relationship are different, but that should not negate your level of respect for the other parent.

## Communication Between Parent and Child/Children

A chief complaint that I receive as an attorney is that one co-parent is not able to communicate with the child while they are with the other co-parent. If your children are old enough to have a cell phone, just buy it. It cuts down on the back-and-forth bickering. It also minimizes the frequency of having to speak with your former partner daily.

It's hard to heal from your divorce or breakup when you constantly have to communicate with the other co-parent. It is even more challenging to heal when you still have to deal with the same disrespect. I would suggest that if one co-parent has a hard time letting go and needs to speak with the children nearly every day, then it may be wise to set times for them to communicate with the child. While it's understandable that being away from your child(ren) is all new, the other co-parent still needs to enjoy quality time with the child(ren) without having tons of interruptions.

## Parenting Styles

It's important to recognize at the beginning of the separation, divorce, or breakup that your parenting style will likely be different from the other co-parent's parenting style. In a perfect world, having a sit-down conversation with the child(ren) about the expectations at each house would be ideal. It would be even better if co-parents could get on the same page with how you all intend to raise the child(ren). Unfortunately, your co-parent relationship may not be at a mature level yet. So, to keep you from going insane, just mentally prepare yourself to have to re-teach the child/children each time they come back to your place.

I also encourage you to have some patience and grace with your babies. It's already hard enough that they have to deal with the separation or divorce, but now they have to remember the rules and laws at each parent's house on top of the pressure of just being a child. It will be a lot for them to endure. Be kind and love them as often as you can.

## Boundaries

Learning and implementing boundaries will be instrumental in your healthy co-parent relationship. If you decide to move on to a new relationship shortly after the divorce or breakup, please be mindful of how that may impact the child(ren). They are still trying to grasp the thought of Mom and Dad not living in the same household, let alone meeting your new partner.

It would be amazing if you and the co-parent could have a sit-down about introducing the new partner to the children before they are actually introduced. Now, let me say this: you can't force it. If one co-parent wants to introduce the new partner to the child(ren) without any regard to how the child(ren) will receive it, then they better be ready for the consequences of what the child(ren) may say.

What's equally important to note is that the success of your post-divorce or breakup journey will be contingent on the success of your co-parenting relationship. In other words, if you have a stressful co-parenting relationship, then this will certainly put a strain on your new life post-divorce/breakup. So, it is imperative that you strive to create boundaries that will put you in a position of success.

An issue that I frequently see as a divorce lawyer is that the new partners are actively involved in the parental decisions. While this is admirable, one should be cognizant of the impact that this could have on the former partner and children. In the early stages of a new relationship, it is best to use wisdom and keep the new partners out of all parental decisions.

## Relationship Between Parents

The relationship between you and your former partner did not work, but that does not mean that the co-parenting relationship can't be a success. I have noticed that some people take the divorce or breakup really hard, and they intentionally make the other co-parent's life a living hell. I've seen it time and time again. If that's you on the receiving end, I encourage you to hang in there. Secondly, I encourage you to keep everything documented because you will likely end up back in court. Lastly, being nice goes a long way. If one co-parent requests to make changes to the schedule, then please consider it and be flexible. Why? Because I can almost guarantee that you will need to do the same at some point.

# AFFIRMATION

I have a healthy co-parent relationship.

My patience and communication skills with my co-parent will continuously improve.

My co-parent's patience and communication skills with me will continuously improve.

I will be respectful to my co-parent's new partner.

My co-parent will be respectful to me and my new partner.

My co-parent and I will not involve the child(ren) in adult matters.

My co-parent and I will not use the child(ren) as a pawn.

My co-parent and I will follow any and all court orders and will stay out of court.

My co-parent and I will do what's best for the children and put our differences aside, always.

My co-parent relationship has healthy boundaries.

My children will not be negatively impacted by the divorce or breakup, no matter what the statistics say.

I have a successful blended family.

My blended family is a success story to model after!

# XI. FINANCIAL MATTERS

## Lawyer Fees and Cost to Fight

There's one thing that I know for certain about every divorce, no matter what state you are in: Each person is impacted financially by the divorce process. From the court costs to the lawyer fees, it all adds up, and it's not fun.

One of the first things that I believe is crucial for anyone going through a divorce or anyone who has just experienced a divorce is to determine what is really important to you. Most of the time, I find that people just fight to prove themselves right, when that does absolutely nothing for your case. Even if you have already experienced a divorce with children, I can't tell you the number of times I've seen people end up back in court once the case was finalized. They want to continue the fight. This fight is exhausting and is a waste of financial resources.

The cost of litigation adds up quickly, and once you look up, you could have had a nice chunk of change in your savings account rather than spend it fighting with your former partner. If your children are most important to you in this fight, then I strongly urge you to figure out what is really best for them. Not best from an emotional point of view, but best based on the laws of your state. Most states have "best interest factors." I always tell my clients and potential clients that this is the court's bible when it comes to custody cases, so you need to know what you have to prove to prevent you from making irrelevant arguments in court.

Most of the time, when wives/mothers are fighting the husbands/fathers for custody, it's because they believe that the children would be better suited living with them. I often ask the wives/mothers why they feel this way, and usually, not always, the response is that because the husband/father is not responsible enough to have a 50/50 arrangement. I usually respond by telling the wives/mothers that if you don't give him an opportunity to try and be the best father, then you are right; he won't be responsible enough because he has not been afforded the opportunity.

I've found that, more often than not, once 50/50 custody is ordered by the judge, the same wives and mothers who initially thought it was the worst decision eventually came back to me, admitting it wasn't as bad as they had imagined. Having split custody has given them a chance to live a little. I've always encouraged those wives/mothers to start a 50/50 custody arrangement on a temporary basis and see how it goes. Document how it works for everyone. Sometimes, the outcome can be surprising. If it isn't successful and the father drops the ball, then there's relevant evidence that can be used in court.

Now, let me be clear: I'm not saying that 50/50 is always best because that's not my belief. I believe that each case should be looked at individually, and the facts should be appropriately applied to the law. There have been some instances where 50/50 was not the best, and I've fought to prove that in court. The point is to figure out what really matters to you and during the process, ask yourself if you could live with the worst possible scenario.

For the mothers/wives who desire majority custody, I tell them that their worst day in court is 50/50 custody. After hearing this, some can live with that decision, and some can't. For the wives/mothers who decide that they want to fight it out, they usually end up needing more financial assistance from family and friends because it costs money to continue the fight in court.

## How Not to Spend So Much on Lawyer Fees?

As of the writing of this book, it's been eight years of owning and operating a law firm. So, I've had an opportunity to assess which types of clients spend the most money on lawyer fees. I'm not an expert in this, but this is my observation. The top three categories of individuals who I believe spend the most on lawyer fees are:

1. People who are extremely impulsive

2. People who are extremely emotional

3. People who like to be right all the time

First, let's talk about impulsive people. These are the potential clients who call the law office, and after ten minutes of speaking to our office, they immediately hire us. Now, there's nothing wrong with this if the individual has already done their due diligence and was ready to hire. I'm not referring to those types of people.

I'm referring to people who have just gotten into an argument with their partner or the other parent, and they want to act immediately because of the incident. They usually don't give much thought to the cost of what it will take to file a case and hire a lawyer. Sometimes, these are the same people who end up dismissing their case at a later time, or the case just drags on for months, if not years, because they weren't really ready to file a case but were just acting impulsively.

Second, you have extremely emotional people. These are the potential clients who will call you every time something happens. I'm not talking about things that are legal and helpful to the case. I'm talking about anything non-legal. For example, the soon-to-be ex verbally called you out of your name during an argument, but you were not threatened or physically harmed. The school allowed the child to be picked up early by the dad, and you want to know what action we can take against the school. The new partner is showing up to the child's games and is staring at you. The list can go on. The point is most of these examples do not help your case.

These are conversations that I would encourage someone to have with their family members and friends and not the lawyer. The minute you contact your lawyer to tell him/her what's been going on, then you are billed for that conversation (presuming the lawyer does billable hours).

Also, I've seen extremely emotional people get so frustrated and irritated with the court process that they refuse to follow the required steps. For example, most states require financial disclosures in a divorce or custody case. I would say that 98.999% hate this part of the process. Frankly, I don't like it either. However, it's part of the process.

Instead of the individual doing what they need to do to comply with the financial disclosure, they don't comply at all. Then, the lawyer's office has to repeatedly contact the individual for the financial documents. I've also seen individuals only partially comply with the financial disclosures. Then, the lawyer's office has to send emails requesting the remaining missing documents.

All of this back and forth starts to add up in lawyer fees. It would be simple and cost-effective if the individual organized their documents and provided all of the information that is needed... the first go-round. That way, it eliminates the lawyer's office from having to review the file constantly and follow up.

Third, you have people who always want to be right. The desire to want to be right all of the time is going to cost you. Sometimes, playing smarter, not saying much, and speaking when the time is right will help you immensely. I see that happen a lot when people want to argue their case at the very beginning stages. Frequently, I remind clients that there is a step-by-step process in place, and we will have an opportunity to iron out all of the issues and arguments related to supporting case law or statutes. Remember, there is a time and place for everything. You will have your day in court if the case does not settle, so there is no need to try and prove yourself every step of the way.

Now, I'm a crybaby as well. I am extremely emotional. Luckily, I represented myself in my divorce case, so I didn't pay for lawyer fees. I don't want you to feel attacked because that's not the point of me mentioning these types of people. The point I'm trying to make is that there are lawyers who love to see these types of people walk through their doors. Do you know why? Because it screams billable hours.

The more you talk to your lawyer (if your lawyer is billable), the more money they will make. Unfortunately, it's these kinds of people who are preyed on by money-hungry lawyers. I always tell clients at the very beginning of the legal representation that it's not that I don't desire to talk to them, but my goal is to have your financial interest in mind. The more we communicate, the more you will be charged. Some clients like to communicate with their lawyers on a weekly basis. If there is nothing scheduled, such as a court hearing, a deposition, a mediation, etc., chances are, there is no need to communicate. Now, if something comes up that is helpful to the case, then that's an exception.

The takeaway is that you have some control over how much money you spend with your lawyer. Be wise in how often you communicate and follow the step-by-step process. Most of the time, people who do this don't end up paying the arm and the leg that we often hear about.

## From Two Incomes to One

Naturally, one would think that going from a two-person household to a one-person household would set them behind financially. I have found that not to be true. From my observation, people who have divorced or broken up after living together were spending their money frivolously. Most couples were not maximizing their incomes to live a better life; that's why a lot of them divorced because of financial reasons. I observed that there is usually one person who is really financially savvy, and the other person is the big spender. If you were like me, I was the financially savvy partner.

When I divorced, my finances were in the worst condition that they had ever been. My savings were low, and my debts were high. Not only that, but my credit score was suffering. This is the case for a lot of divorced or soon-to-be divorced individuals, so please do not feel alone.
I often have to review financial affidavits, credit reports, bank statements, and credit card statements, and I was not alone in this regard.

While I was separated, it was important to me not to take out any additional debt and to begin saving. I was a little apprehensive about doing this because I knew that if I didn't file for a divorce, my hard work would go to waste because until the divorce was filed, all of my assets and debts were still considered marital property. So, I made sure that I filed for divorce and then aggressively got back on track financially once the divorce was initiated and after it was completed.

Having one income forces you to spend differently. You no longer have that disposable income that you had become accustomed to. Now, you actually have to watch every penny that you spend and only spend money on items that are needed. During this time, I also made sure that I was living within my means. If I couldn't pay cash for items, then I refused to charge them. Becoming disciplined in this area allowed me to pay off my credit card debt and my vehicle.

Don't feel ashamed to return to your parent's home or get a roommate. In February 2019, when my former partner told me that he was moving out, I didn't know what I was going to do. At that time, I was only in business for a little over two years and was paying myself roughly $1500… on a good month! My whopping $1500 would barely cover my monthly living expenses. In fact, I believe that I was reporting a deficit on my financial affidavit when I filed it in court.

Thankfully, a friend asked to move into my one-bedroom apartment. The goal was for her to stay with me for only six months. She moved into my apartment in March 2019. She ended up staying longer and moved out in December 2020. This was a blessing for both of us because it allowed us to cut our living expenses and save more. We became financial accountability partners, ensuring that we were not excessively spending. We would meet on a monthly basis to discuss our finances.

It is not uncommon for people to move back to their parents' house or to find a roommate after a divorce. This is especially true when one of the partners is solely dependent on the other. In my case, although I was highly educated and was a licensed attorney, it took a while to get a business running and generating good profit. I was in a new state and literally was building a business from the ground up with no prior experience. I had never owned or operated anything. I had $500 and a dream— that's it.

## Set New Financial Goals as a Single Person

At this very stage of your life, I would encourage you to sit down and write out all of your assets, debts, income, and expenses. If you have filed for a divorce already, then use the financial affidavit that you filed in court as a guide. If you have not filed for divorce yet but plan to file soon, then this is a great exercise for you because you will need to complete this task for your divorce.

It's important for you to do this because you need to see where you are financially and make a commitment to turn your financial picture around. Set goals to gradually pay off debt, how much money you want to save, how much money you want to make, and even consider creating new streams of income. New streams of income do not have to be another full-time job, but it can be something as simple as creating content on social media or driving Uber for extra cash.

For me, I wanted to start by paying off my credit card, then my private student loan, and my car note. My ultimate goal was to own a home, but in order to do that, I had to make more money and eliminate debt. When I first applied for a home loan in 2019, the same year as my separation and divorce, I was turned down. However, I didn't walk away with nothing. I obtained valuable information to help me on my financial journey. That included applying for the income-based student loan forgiveness program and eliminating my debt. I worked on these matters for several years. Unfortunately, COVID-19 created a bit of a setback because the business was slower, but I never gave up. Eventually, in April 2023, my goal was realized when I purchased my first property in Florida.

# AFFIRMATION

I have fully recovered financially from my divorce or breakup.
I have more money now than I did when I was married or in a relationship.
The judge will be a righteous judge who follows the law and is fair.
The judge will be well-prepared and kind.
My attorney will be someone of integrity who has good ethics.
My attorney will follow the law and will give ME sound legal advice.
The attorney's prices will align with my budget, and they
will not overcharge me for their services.
My attorney-client relationship will be seamless. I will have sufficient funds to
continue the attorney-client relationship.
My attorney-client relationship will be built on trust, and it will be a great working
relationship where I feel heard and understood.
My attorney and I will operate as a team.
My soon-to-be former spouse or former partner will cooperate during the process
by providing full financial disclosure of assets, debts, income, and expenses.
All hidden or concealed assets, debts, income, and expenses will be revealed to me.
There will be no unnecessary delays, and if delays do arise, they will benefit me.
My legal outcome will be fair.
When I feel overwhelmed by the court process, I will realign and remember to
trust the process.

# XII. REST

Why is it so difficult for some of us to rest? I really wish that I had the answer to this question. Society has trained us to believe that we will be more successful if we do not rest. You often hear "successful" people talk about how early they get up and how late they go to bed. Not getting rest is almost glorified. I wholeheartedly disagree with this concept.

Although I find it extremely difficult to rest, I do recognize how important it is to do it. Not only do I find it difficult to rest, but I begin to feel guilty when I rest. Oftentimes, if I'm on a break trying to rest and control my thoughts, I struggle with turning my brain completely off and just living in the moment. This is also true when I attempt to sleep. Some nights, I think so much about what I have to do the next day that I even start to dream about cases or judges.

I know that some of you deal with this same problem. I can say this with certainty based on how often I receive emails from clients. Some clients email at 2 am, 3 am, etc. This is usually an indicator that the client was not resting but wrestling with their thoughts and experiencing anxiety about the outcome of their case. Then, at times, the late emails turn into text messages or phone calls because the client is unable to rest.

The process of separation and divorce is mentally taxing and takes a toll on you. The thought of you resting is usually not a top priority. The main focus during this phase is usually the thought of you adjusting to living life without your partner. From personal experience, one of the hardest parts of this phase for me was going to bed alone. I had become so accustomed to sleeping on a particular side of the bed and knowing that I was never alone at home.

I remember when my separation first began, I started to have a change in my appetite, and I could not sleep throughout the night. I was so afraid that I would have a hard time sleeping and eating and would fall into depression that I went to see a medical professional. At the appointment, I explained that I was going through a separation and was experiencing a decreased appetite and lack of sleep.

I was diagnosed with situational depression and prescribed medicine. I attempted to take the medicine to help cope with the loss of appetite and insomnia, but I eventually stopped taking it because of the side effects. Since I decided to discontinue my medication, I found an alternative to help me sleep, and that was YouTube videos. I would find powerful prayers to listen to until I dozed off, or I would listen to the sound of rain to ease my mind until I fell asleep. I did this for several weeks until I was able to sleep on my own. As for my appetite, once I began to seek therapy and work on the issues that were causing me the most stress and anxiety, my appetite returned.

## Benefits of Resting

I do not claim to be a doctor because I'm not, so I will not state the medical benefits of resting. However, from my personal experience and from observing others, when we have had a great night's rest, we feel refreshed and rejuvenated. On the flip side, if we did not have enough rest the night before, we typically are sluggish. When we get adequate rest, we become more refreshed and think clearly. Even if you drink caffeine regularly, it does not compare to how well your mind and body will feel after getting adequate rest.

Some of us are working men and women, and our jobs or business(es) require us to show up each and every day at 100%. Honestly, it is not a realistic expectation, but it is the expectation nonetheless. It is difficult to function and perform at your highest potential if you are lacking rest.

As you begin to create your new normal—life after divorce, I need you to make resting a new routine. It needs to be an intentional act. I know what society has trained us to believe, but my goal is for us to live above societal norms. To create our own culture where we can grow and thrive on our terms. You will not be able to grow and thrive if you do not rest!

## Cons of Not Resting

Have you ever dealt with a toddler who was extremely exhausted but refused to go to sleep? Yeah, me too. They cry, fall out, and constantly whine. For adults, our exhaustion is not too different. Sometimes, we cry because the daily stress of life feels never-ending. When we lack proper rest, I notice that we tend to bleed on to others unintentionally. Sometimes, this takes the form of being too harsh to our children for minor things or snapping at family and friends because they have triggered us in some way. Usually, these moments that cause us to snap would not bother us in any other circumstance. However, remember that your divorce process has a different impact on you, and most people will not understand unless they have experienced something similar.

In these moments when your social battery tank is low and you are feeling exhausted from lack of sleep, I would encourage you to give your loved ones a heads-up. Just ask them to be mindful of your situation and have some compassion. Because they love you, they will hear you and likely acquiesce. Give yourself permission to be mentally, physically, and emotionally exhausted and just REST!

# AFFIRMATION

I need rest.
It's OK to rest.
I will not feel guilty about resting.
I will make resting a priority.
When I rest, I will feel refreshed and re-energized.

# XIII. NEW BEGINNINGS

## New Beginnings

After being separated for several months, I never forgot the day that I found my strength and felt happy. This was the first time I had joy in a long time. It was on July 5, 2019. A few nights before, I had written down some ideas about how my new life would be. There were several categories in my journal, including:

1) Travel
2) Living arrangements
3) Business, etc…just to name a few.

Under each category, I started to write out what I envisioned for myself. Under travel, I wanted to go to Africa. I had never gone before, and it had been on my bucket list since I was a child. For living arrangements, I wanted to decorate my apartment in a cute and sophisticated manner but on a budget. For the first time in my entire adulthood, I was preparing to live by myself. It was exciting yet scary at the same time. For business, I wanted to make more money because, at that time, I was only paying myself $1500 per month. I couldn't do much with that.

Designing my new life was the positive mental shift that I needed to help me focus on my future rather than my past. I was ready to live an abundant life on my terms. I didn't have to consider anyone else's thoughts or suggestions; I could just live for myself. I'm certain that this mental shift is what helped me begin to see life differently. It was during this time that I went from being a victim to being victorious. I no longer felt defeated and was ready to see what life had to offer me.

## Let's Redesign Your New Life

Now, this is the fun part. Here, we get to imagine a completely new life. This life will be filled with positivity, wealth, peace, and lots of happiness. When I was in life coaching to cope with my divorce, one of my assignments was to write out five fun places that I had never gone to but desired to visit. Then, I had to put these activities on the calendar and eventually go to these places. This task sounds so easy to some, but for the overthinkers, the givers, and the ones who like to put themselves last, this task will be more difficult than it sounds.

I cannot begin to express to you how liberating the assignment was for me. It was so freeing that I started giving out this same homework assignment to my divorce clients. One client wrote out her list in 2021. Then, years after her divorce was finalized, she reached out to me and told me that she completed a lot of items on her list. She was a completely different person than the woman that I had met years prior.

This assignment will help you reflect on your life to see how far you have come. Right now, while you are in pain, you may not see or know how soon you will get out of it. The journey seems long and lonely. Fortunately for you, months from now, you will look back to appreciate how far you have come. I promise, you will not look the same, nor will you feel the same. I can't tell you how many times people told me that I was glowing once I started to enjoy and trust the journey. I would not trade my journey for anyone or anything.

## Change the Scenery

During my separation, divorce, and after the divorce, I was still living in the same apartment that my former spouse and I lived in during the marriage. As part of our settlement agreement, I told him that he could take most of the major furniture in the place. I've always had the mindset that I would rebuild and start from ground zero. And that's exactly what I did.

When he moved out of that one-bedroom apartment, my place was nearly empty. I didn't even have a bed to my name, but I was completely okay with that because what I wasn't going to do was beg anyone, especially him, to help me rebuild. My thought process was that I always excelled under pressure, so this trial was no different than any other trial that I had experienced.

I went into Rooms to Go and found several furniture items that I liked. I financed the items and made payments on them until it was paid in full. I will never forget when the furniture was delivered to my apartment. I felt powerful. This was motivation to set another goal and complete it.

Changing my environment helped me tremendously with healing from my divorce because I didn't have much furniture to remind me of our marriage. I tend to operate as an "out of sight, out of mind" person. That's what works for me. Making my apartment my very own was the steppingstone to eventually purchasing my first home years later.

## Now, Go Be Great…On Purpose!

As I close, I want you to know that you have everything within you to live a healthy, fulfilling, and prosperous life. There are no limits to how successful you can be. I want you to win and attain everything that your heart desires.

I hope this book has uplifted, empowered, and encouraged you to be the best version of yourself!

NOW…GO live your life authentically and unapologetically…on PURPOSE!

# AFFIRMATION

I live my life with intention.
My future is brighter than my past.
I create peaceful environments.
I find solace in my new life.
I AM great…on purpose!

# ACKNOWLEDGMENTS

This book is a testament that you can survive any storm and thrive! I am happy that I pushed beyond my fears to write this book.

To my siblings - J.C. and Mondy, thank you for putting up with me all of these years. I am the baby, and for years, I have been giving you both a run for your money. To have two siblings who have my back no matter what and who always support me is priceless.

To my friends since childhood—Nasea and Shaunda, I love y'all to pieces. It doesn't matter how far I move or how long we go without speaking; I know that you guys are always there.

To my college bro—Caleb, you have been my bonus brother, whom I cherish with every fiber in me.

To my two friends with the same name - Andre—I appreciate you both. Both of you tell me what I need to hear and give me much wisdom in times of distress.

To my line sister and friend - Dr. Sheena, I love you and appreciate our girlfriend chats.

To my Florida girlfriends—Sadarria and Crystal, y'all have held me down for years, and I probably would not have stayed in Florida as long as I have if it weren't for the two of you.

To Mama Judge Daniels and brother Reece, the love y'all give me is priceless. I deeply appreciate being a part of the family.

To my family - each of you has supported me throughout my life, and because of you, I am wiser and better.

To my YT – you get on my last nerve, but you know it's all love. I appreciate our friendship.

To my second Mom - Mom Cynthia (RIP), I love and miss you so much. Your fervent prayers have kept me.

To Alejandra Zilak, Esq. – I love and appreciate you so much. Thanks for helping me edit this book. I value your opinion and feedback.

To my publishing company - Beyond The Book Media. I thank you for your prayers, your patience, your integrity, and your professionalism. I could not have birthed this book without you all.

Lastly, I would like to extend a heartfelt thank you to my former clients and current clients. I would not be the attorney I am today without you all. You all have believed in me and trusted me in your darkest hours. For that, I am grateful!

# REBUILDING YOUR LIFE

## ——AFTER A——
# DIVORCE/BREAKUP
### THE DIVORCE LAWYER'S PERSPECTIVE

Rebuilding Your Life After a Divorce/Breakup: The Divorce Lawyer's Perspective is a motivational and inspirational book to help men and women experiencing a breakup or divorce transition into their singleness. It provides practical tips for cultivating healthy co-parent relationships. It also assists men and women in discovering themselves and finding joy in the journey as they transition into their newness. Lastly, this book uplifts, encourages, and inspires individuals who have a family law custody battle by providing practical tips.

Shamika T. Askew, Esquire, is a licensed attorney in the States of Michigan and Florida. She has a virtual law firm focusing on family law (divorce, child custody, and child support) and personal injury (car accidents and slips & falls). She is a passionate lawyer who desires to see families heal from their divorce and breakups. She is also an inspirational and motivational speaker and author.

Learn more about Shamika on her website: www.shamikataskew.com.

www.ingramcontent.com/pod-product-compliance
Lightning Source LLC
La Vergne TN
LVHW052038080426
835513LV00018B/2386